# LIFE IS A SQUIGGLY LINE

# LIFE IS A *Squiggly* LINE

START EMBRACING IMPERFECTION AND STOP SETTLING FOR SAFE

FALLON UKPE

WALNUT & SAGE



LIFE IS A SQUIGGLY LINE
*Start Embracing Imperfection and Stop Settling for Safe*

ISBN 978-1-5445-0556-5 *Hardcover*
978-1-5445-0554-1 *Paperback*
978-1-5445-0555-8 *Ebook*

*To God—*

*Thank you for all that I am, all that I have, and all that I give.*

*Thank you for filling me with a purpose and a desire to live a life in service of others.*

*To Mom, Dad, and Shelter—*

*Thank you for loving me and supporting me always, no matter what.*

*I could not have asked for a better family.*

# CONTENTS

# INTRODUCTION

## HOW IT ALL STARTED

I was wrestling with what to say. I had nearly four months to plan for this, but still, I had nothing prepared. At the start of the year, I accepted an invitation as a guest speaker at an event for a group of talented and brilliant undergraduate women. Now, summer had arrived, the event was the next day, and I still wasn't even close to being ready.

I had a few tidbits and pieces of advice that I thought I could share. But there was nothing concrete—no outline, no plan, no written remarks. I was struggling to find the right words, the right message. I wanted to be the *perfect* balance of funny and inspiring, wise yet approachable, accomplished but still relatable. And somehow, the harder I thought about it and pushed myself to craft the *perfect* speech with just the right delivery, the more elusive it became.

So, I decided to sleep on it. The event wasn't until tomorrow morning, so surely a night's rest would be helpful. And maybe by thinking about it just before bed, I would somehow wake up with a flash of inspiration. I turned off the lights and quickly fell asleep. All too soon, I heard the sound of my alarm. I turned to the side to silence it, and I saw the morning light shining in the windows. I looked back to check the time. I had an hour before I needed to start getting ready. I scanned my brain for an answer to my dilemma. But nothing. I panicked (briefly!) then sprang into action.

I shot out of bed and went down to my office. I had to figure it out. I took a few clean sheets of paper out of the printer and picked up my favorite pen. I began to just let my mind roam while holding my hand above the paper. It was my full-on, clean-sheet brainstorming mode. I scribbled a few words and phrases, yet still, nothing hit me.

I looked up at the ceiling and then back down at my desk. I glanced to the left and saw some notes partially hidden under a few folders. I had just written a note to a family friend's daughter who was graduating from college. I carefully slid the note out from the bottom of the pile and moved it to the center of my desk. I scanned the paper and a small drawing that I had added in the middle of her letter caught my eye. Ha, there it was. That drawing was my speech. But I had to figure out a few more things, get dressed, and drive to the event.

I was running short on time. I quickly got ready and rushed to the car. I exited my driveway and made a few turns heading toward the 400 southbound highway. I drove in silence. I was trying to work through those last loose ends of the speech. As I merged onto the freeway, my brain was abuzz as different thoughts and ideas trickled in. Yet, I felt an odd sense of calm. My gaze focused on the road ahead as I whizzed past skyscrapers, overpasses, and exit signs.

And then—suddenly—it came to me. That was it! The last few pieces I needed to make it all work lit up my brain like quick flashes. I felt a sense of relief and excitement. I exited the freeway and began looking for street parking. Mentally, I ran through the speech one more time. As I turned left onto Ellis Street and parked at the meter, my phone buzzed. Two of my friends (who were also coordinating the event) were waiting for me in the lobby. I quickly hopped out of the car, paid the meter, and rounded the street corner toward the building.

About twenty minutes later, I headed into the room where

everyone was seated. It was go time. After a brief introduction by a close friend, I began. I passed around empty sheets of white printer paper to each audience member. I asked them to use the paper and a pen to finish the sentence "Life is..." in less than three minutes. While they labored over capturing the depth and breadth of life's meaning onto one page in just a few minutes, I stepped to the side and quickly scribbled down my own answer in less than four seconds. Though, to be fair, I did have several months, the morning, and a car ride to figure it out.

A few minutes later, I asked for volunteers to share their papers. The responses were beautiful, profound, and amazing. I was in awe and truly blown away at the range of responses and ways they had chosen to express them, and I wasn't the only one. The audience was, too. They cheered and applauded for each woman who shared her page. After hearing from several audience members, I returned to the front of the room. I commended the group for their creativity and thanked the volunteers for sharing their work. Then, I told them that I wanted to share mine.

I picked up my paper and held it up with the drawing facing the audience.

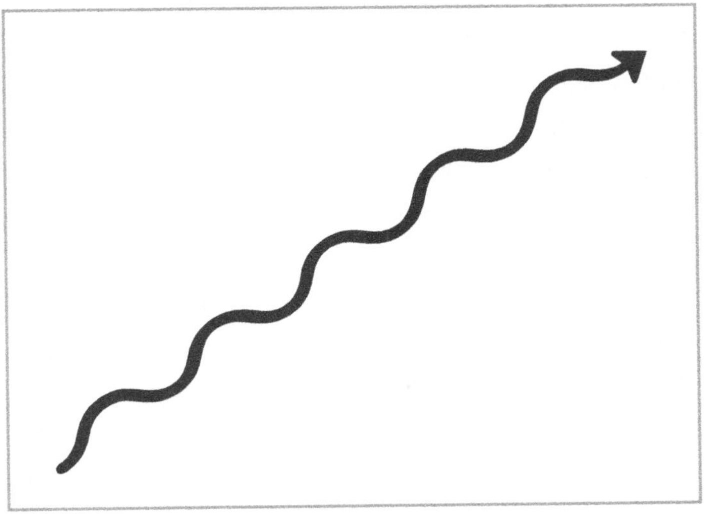

Smiling, I said, "Life is a squiggly line."

I explained that the squiggly line meant that life would not be perfect, and there would be ups and downs; but in the end, it would all work out if they took charge of the journey and focused on growing through the experiences.

What followed was an amazing thirty minutes of storytelling (from me) and lots of laughter (from a room of incredibly talented women). After my speech, there were several questions from the audience; their questions led to an incredible dialogue on topics ranging from dealing with Imposter's Syndrome to what I wish I knew at their age and stage of life. Days after that talk, I received an influx of messages and connection requests via LinkedIn. I was humbled and energized. Somehow in sharing my story—even the rough, not-so-neatly-planned parts—I had struck a chord with an entire room of people. I received emails from women who expressed that the lessons and stories I shared were invaluable to them. One even promised that she would always remember to own her squiggly.

I believed that if the message had resonated so much with that audience, I was obligated to figure out how to share it more broadly. So, I began to think that writing a book could be the best way to capture and share my thoughts. But it was a scary proposition. I had never imagined I could be an author of an *entire* book. So, I tabled the idea.

Then, months later, I decided it might not be such a silly idea. I had been journaling one afternoon, and the thought of the book resurfaced. And I had ideas about what I actually wanted to write. So, I quickly created a book outline. It took less than an hour. Somehow, it was all flowing through the tip of my pen as I hurriedly wrote chapter topics and stories, trying to keep up with my brain. Over the next few weeks, I would look back at the notes and second-guess whether I could really be an author and write a book.

Then, one day, I just started. On a cold evening in late October, I was flipping through my old journal. I came across the book outline and the notes. I reread them, smiling. That smile transformed into an unrelenting urge to just start writing. So, I opened my laptop, opened a blank document in Word, and I began to write. In fact, the first thing that I wrote was this introduction.

And now, about one year later, I am sharing the finished product with you. *Life Is A Squiggly Line* will discuss how to embrace imperfection, stop settling for safe, and own your squiggly (your path forward). By sharing the lessons I have learned along my squiggly line, my hope is that it helps others avoid the same mistakes and inspires others to live more fully. I've also created additional free tools to help you along the journey that are available on the *www.OwnYourSquiggly.com* website.

I believe that we are each completely unique individuals with innate talents and strengths that the world needs. If we each make the most of our squiggly line and maximize the use of our unique talents during our lives, we will leave this place far better than when we arrived, experience life as an incredible adventure, and create a collective legacy that positively impacts the world around us—perhaps for generations to come.

So, let's embark on this journey together. Choose to embrace imperfection. Choose to stop settling for safe. Choose to own your squiggly. Let me help you get there, and you'll never look back.

*Part One*

# EMBRACING IMPERFECTION

*Chapter One*

# THE MYTH OF PERFECTION

"How many of you like rollercoasters?" I asked. More than half the room raised their hands.

"Okay, put your hands down. This isn't for you all," I quipped. Everyone laughed.

"How many of you *don't* like rollercoasters?" I asked, and this time, I raised my hand, too. We all laughed again.

"Yes—*these* are my people!" I exclaimed with a smile. "So, life is a squiggly line, and that squiggly line feels like a rollercoaster," I began to explain.

I was beginning my speech to an audience of bright, talented undergraduate women, and I had just revealed my definition of life to the room: the squiggly line. So, what exactly is the "squiggly line"? Glad you asked. Here's my definition:

> *The squiggly line is the journey in front of any individual or organization that takes them from current state to a future state.*
>
> *Furthermore, the journey is imperfect and, at times, unpredictable. Nonetheless, if one properly defines the end-state vision, owns the actions along the journey's path, and embraces imperfection, it will lead to success, impact, and fulfillment.*

How exactly does the squiggly line relate to life? I'll explain by first talking about the squiggly line's opposite: the straight line.

Many of us plan for a trajectory that is a straight line up and to the right, just like this:

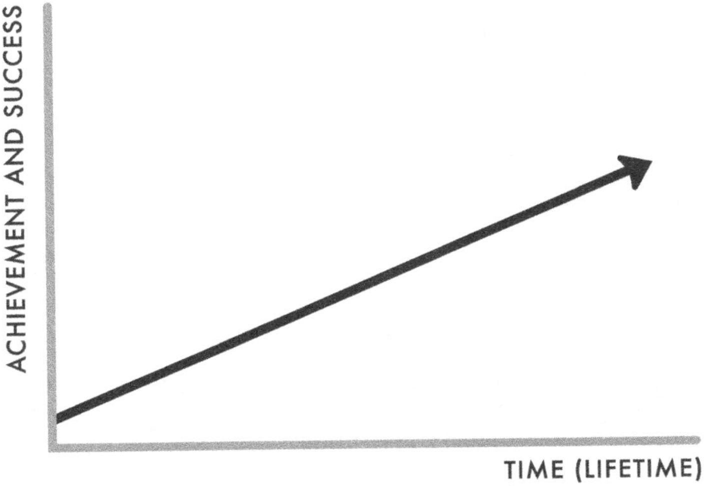


We expect linear progress and growth, with the achievement of major milestones—graduating college, big promotions at work, marriage, children, or other key markers of "progression"—that happen at *just* the right time. For the record, I had always been one of those people, and I still sometimes succumb to trying to plan aspects of my life this way, even though I know better.

Not only do we plan and expect this in our personal lives, we also plan and expect it in our professional endeavors as well. We want—and expect—our businesses or ventures to grow at a strong, positive rate. Heck, sometimes we curve up the tail on the right, denoting *exponential* growth.

And when we look at successful people, we assume that their path has to be—yes, you guessed it—a straight line trajectory that is up and to the right. What's even worse is that we tend to reject or negatively respond when anything isn't a path straight up and to the right. In other words, we irrationally expect complete and utter perfection.

Well, Houston, we have a problem. In fact, we have *three* problems: first, perfection is unattainable; second, perfection is unfulfilling; and third, perfection is unnecessary. Let's take a moment to break that all down.

### PERFECTION IS UNATTAINABLE

Somehow, we have been programmed to believe that the line of life is a perfect trajectory up and to the right, but that just isn't possible. Perfection is impossible. So, we are effectively in pursuit of something that simply does not exist, living our lives on a hamster wheel of sorts.

Unfortunately, that type of quest is typically driven from a place of fear, inadequacy, or both. The fear is often a fear of failure or a fear of what people will think if we do (or don't do) something. That fear is also what drives us to settle for safe rather than go after something that we truly want. Inadequacy is often from feeling like we are not enough. That often manifests as a belief that we have to prove ourselves to others to be accepted, liked, respected, or loved. There can also be other causes for feelings of inadequacy. The short list I provided here just names some of the common ones.

Those negative feelings—fear and inadequacy—are usually buried deep down. They usually aren't things we readily understand are driving our actions. So, you might be wondering where those feelings come from. Well, those feelings are typically the result of certain experiences that we encounter and subsequently, the perspectives that we adopt. Here's what I mean: Somewhere along our own journey, we experienced something or were told something that triggered those feelings. And for many people, it happened several times, not just once. That repeated triggering sent signals and messages that stuck with us and altered our thought patterns. And those thoughts turned into beliefs that we adopted and now carry around with us.

It's important to recognize that the beliefs that we developed as a result of negative experiences are *learned*. That's not truly who we are, nor do I believe that those false beliefs should dictate how we live. It's critical that we go back to the core of who we each are and strip away all of the external labels and judgments and beliefs—especially those that have led to a sense of fear and inadequacy. We need a hard reset to stop living our lives according to a set of false beliefs, and to stop chasing unattainable perfection.

## PERFECTION IS UNFULFILLING

Not only are we chasing something that we cannot achieve, but we are also often trading our happiness for it. Pursuing perfection means that we are on a path doing what looks good and what signals external achievement to the world; however, it isn't likely to be a path that brings us true fulfillment and lasting joy. How does this show up in our lives? It often means that we are working in jobs that do not leverage our unique talents or align with our sense of meaning and purpose. As a result, we often don't look forward to work, which is how we spend the majority of our waking hours each day as adults. Or maybe we do look forward to work for a period of time, but we get bored or frequently feel like we need to make a change. By pursuing perfection and doing what looks good, we wind up feeling drained and unfulfilled because we are chasing the wrong "why."

What do I mean? The crux of the issue in the example that I described above is that the "why" behind what we do is about chasing perfection to help resolve fear and inadequacy. If we continue to do this, then we become unfulfilled. And that's because we live constantly in pursuit of perfection (which we can't actually attain), and we are doing things solely to avoid what scares us or to prove ourselves to other people. It's only natural to feel empty when living life primarily for those reasons. But we have a choice: we can opt out of the hamster wheel and choose to live for a different "why"—one that is about meaning, purpose, and impact.

## PERFECTION IS UNNECESSARY

Quite possibly the worst part of it all is that the pursuit of unattainable and unfulfilling perfection is actually unnecessary. Yet, many of us try to pursue perfection because we believe that it is a precursor to achievement, success, and wealth. And that couldn't be further from the truth.

The most successful people and organizations are imperfect. They have failed. And they'll tell you that the failures were typically the most important moments of their journey.

I challenge you to look up the history of any organization or biography of any individual that you would call "successful." I guarantee that there will be things that they didn't get right, if they are honest and transparent about their journey. And those people (talking about themselves or organizations that they were part of) will usually also tell you that they learned the most when they got it wrong. I know that certainly has been true for me.

Here's the deal: it's not important to get it 100 percent right. What *is* most important is to learn from the times that we don't get it right and to decide that we will continue to grow and persevere through those imperfect moments. And many believe that to truly be successful, imperfection—not just getting it wrong but also the growth from acknowledging it and learning from it—is essential.

Can we agree that it's time to choose a different way to do things? It's time to stop living in the myth of perfection. It's time to choose a life that is meaningful and fulfilling. It's time to choose the squiggly line.

But just in case you still aren't convinced, there's more to why it's time to end the quest for unattainable, unfulfilling, unnecessary perfection.

*Chapter Two*

# CHOOSING THE SQUIGGLY LINE

We talked about the three problems with the myth of perfection and the straight line: it is unattainable, unfulfilling, and unnecessary. If that isn't enough to make you stop pursuing it, there's more. Let's go back to the idea of understanding the straight line versus the squiggly line. You know that they are different shapes, but what you may not have realized is that they are also *completely different trajectories*. Why is that so important? Because it means that choosing one over the other leads to not only a different path but also to a different outcome.

When you look at these lines separately, it may seem that they both get you to the same place.

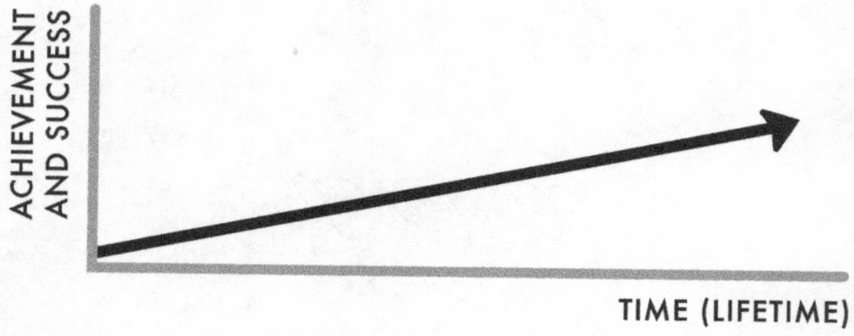


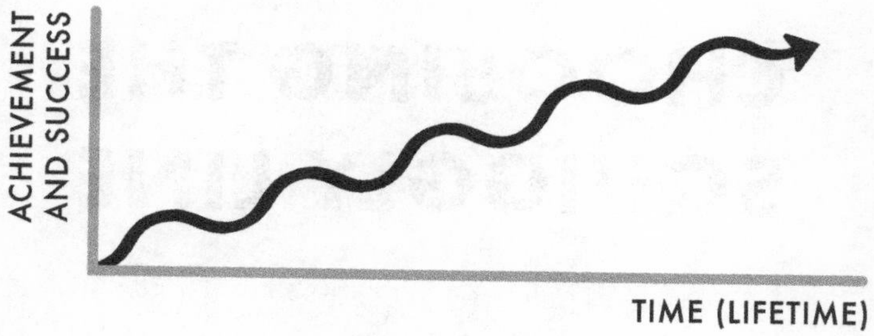


But in reality, they don't. And you can't see that they don't until you map them on the same horizon.

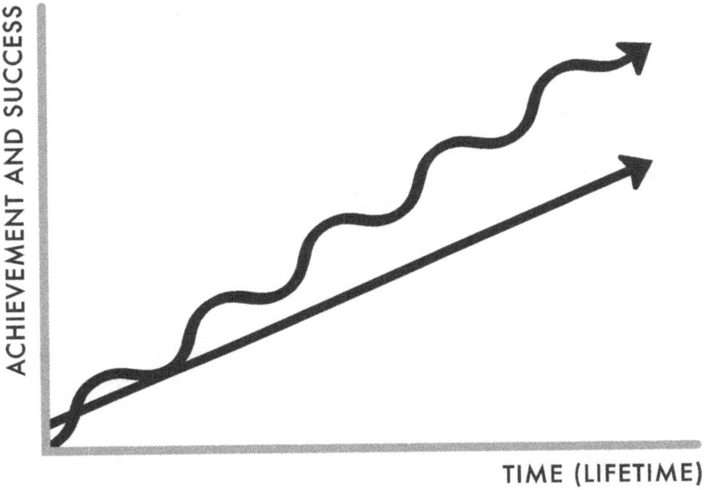


See that? The squiggly line beats the straight line. Why? Because a straight line actually blunts the upward trajectory. It prevents the maximum realization of achievement and success that is meaningful. Let's dive a little deeper by examining the two key measures on the vertical y-axis: achievement and success.

### ACHIEVEMENT

Achievement simply means that a goal or a milestone is attained. In and of itself, an achievement isn't good or bad. It's an achievement. We, ourselves, assign a judgment of value to an achievement. And often, society, family, friends, and others also have a perspective on the value of an achievement. Achievement is limitless on both the squiggly line and the straight line, but there's

### DEFINING KEY TERMS

As I dive more into the differences between the squiggly line and the straight line, there are some key terms that I'll use. These aren't new words. But what is different is how I define them in the context of the squiggly line. I'll weave these in as I move through the deeper dive, but here's a quick, upfront guide with all of the definitions in one place.

- **Achievement:** Attaining a goal or milestone
- **Success:** The ultimate sense of meaning and fulfillment that comes from achieving positive impact by continuously deploying your talents in alignment with your purpose
- **Fulfillment:** A sense of peace and joy from creating a meaningful and purpose-led life that creates positive impact
- **Meaning:** An internally derived sense of self and purpose with a vision for how to navigate your life in alignment with your purpose
- **Purpose:** Clarity on your innate talents and recognition of what we're meant to do in and through our lives

a big difference in what the achievement means to you based on the path that you choose.

The squiggly line is about achievement that is meaningful to you and likely meaningful to others—especially those that are close to you and understand why you decided to pursue that goal or milestone. Said another way, the "why" behind the achievement isn't about pursuing perfection and racking up accolades because that looks good. It's not about resolving feelings of fear or inadequacy. The "why" behind the achievements on the squiggly line is more about who you truly are. It's about milestones that matter because they're part of the vision that you defined for your life. It's about pursuing a path that energizes you and inspires you. It's about the unique imprint that you want to leave in the world.

You may choose to pursue fewer achievements on the squiggly line. Not because you can't do more but because you recognize that you don't need to. You're not driven by meaningless perfection and external applause. Your drive is internal. You're focused on what is purposeful and meaningful and important. You realize that your life is a precious resource to be focused on what matters most.

On the other hand, the straight line is about achievement that is meaningful to others, but not necessarily truly meaningful to you. Some of the achievements may seem great in the moment; however, if you achieved them only to check a box or solely to keep up the myth of perfection, then the excitement quickly fades. Suddenly, you're onto the next big achievement—without even considering if it actually means anything to you—because you're on the hamster wheel of perfection. And this continues. You just keep going until you're left with a bunch of great accolades that only matter when other people see or know about them. And at the end of the day, all that you've really achieved is the creation of an unhappy and unfulfilling life.

This is exactly why many people who have achieved so much and have more financial resources than the overwhelming majority of people living on this planet are still longing for more. How many times have we looked at our own lives (or have we seen someone else examine their own life) to see how much is going "right" and yet there's still dissatisfaction? And what's more is that we're perplexed by the dissatisfaction because, by the "standard" measures of milestones and achievements, we "should" feel like we "have it all." Unfortunately, many people realize this way too late, once they are far down the horizontal x-axis—which represents the finite time resource that we call your life—and often wish for the time back to make different decisions.

Overall, the straight line and the squiggly line tie on the maximum quantitative number of achievements on the graph. However, the squiggly line is far superior in its qualitative value for any achievements that we attain.

## SUCCESS

Success (what I also call *true* success) is the ultimate sense of meaning and fulfillment that comes from achieving positive impact in the lives of others by continuously deploying your talents in alignment with your purpose. Your potential success on the squiggly line is infinite; on the straight line, it is low to non-existent. Success is not about a pile of achievements and accolades that solely or predominately have external meaning—that's what the straight line definition of "success" is. And unfortunately, that's how much of our society and culture views success. But that's not *true* success.

*True* success, as I have defined it above, really begins as an inside job. And the squiggly line recognizes that, but the straight line does not. One of the core parts of success is meaning. Here's the way that I look at meaning: it's an *internally* derived sense of self and purpose with a vision for how to navigate your life in alignment with your purpose. The "inside job" of success begins with you recognizing and defining *for yourself* who you are, what your purpose is, and how you'll lead your life according to your purpose. It has to start with you. If it doesn't, you're on the straight line. And whatever you achieve won't mean much to you. No matter how many achievements, compliments from others, or dollars you accrue, you will not be fulfilled. You will not think that you are truly successful. In fleeting moments, you might. But similar to the issue with achievements on the straight line, you'll be longing for more—for a sense of meaning and fulfillment that only accompanies *true* success.

Success on the squiggly line is infinite because there's an understanding that each person is different for a reason.

You are unique. You are one-of-a-kind. That means that you have a completely different blend of talents, thoughts, and perspectives than any other person on this entire planet. Sure, there may be overlap in what you're able to do and how you perceive things compared to someone else, but it's not *exactly* the same. And that's so important because at the end of the day, your purpose, what gives you meaning, and the impact that you can have in the world will be completely different from the next person. All of this matters because purpose and impact are core to how we experience meaningful success and create a fulfilling life.

The world is waiting on each of us to recognize our innate talents and understand what we are meant to do in and through our lives—that's how I define purpose. Purpose is important for two reasons: first, I believe that living in our purpose allows us to experience a full sense of meaning while providing a clear guide that helps us navigate our life journey; second, I believe that living in our purpose is the pathway to maximizing the positive impact that we can have in the lives of others.

You know, as a matter of fact, the world is not only *waiting* on us to make it better, it *needs* us to make it better. Advances in healthcare to cure diseases, solutions that protect the environment, technologies that enhance global connectivity, ideas that improve our educational systems—all of these innovations and more have to come from *someone*. They have to come from us. Why not you? Our individual scale of impact doesn't need to be large to make a difference. Here's why: if we are all focused on creating a positive impact, then the collective scale of our actions will be enormous.

Coming back to our discussion on success, living in our purpose and creating an impact aren't only important to the world; they're also important to us. Purpose and impact are central to how we experience *true* success while leading a life that is meaningful and fulfilling.

Overall, the squiggly line has infinite success potential while the straight line has little to no success potential. When placed on the graph. the squiggly line is far superior with a much higher possible point on the vertical y-axis.

## THE SQUIGGLY LINE JOURNEY

Now that we have established why and how the squiggly line surpasses the straight line, there's one more part that's important to discuss about the squiggly line. I'm sure you've noticed that the squiggly line has ups and downs—peaks and valleys—rather than just being another straight line with a different endpoint. Let's delve into what that means and why those peaks and valleys are part of the squiggly line journey.

Part of choosing the squiggly line is about accepting that there will be ups and downs—that they are natural parts of the journey. Life isn't perfect, and your path won't be perfect, either. Those ups and downs happen for a reason: they help us grow and become better versions of ourselves while propelling us to more meaningful achievements.

There are countless scientific papers, journal articles, biographies, and anecdotes that show how important it is to have moments where you almost succeed or downright fail. They also show us how those moments positively impact future success. It's been true in my experience, for sure, that getting it wrong has been an invaluable experience. But I've also learned that the positive impact from experiencing setbacks is not merely a given. There's a bit of work that we have to do on our parts: we need to take the time to learn from those moments and incorporate the lessons rather than reacting negatively and trying to avoid future failure at all costs. Whether you believe the science or the real-life anecdotes, it's undeniable that experiencing setbacks is an important teacher. And those moments—represented as dips or valleys on the squiggly line—are part of what propels us forward and upward. So, think of setbacks as life's extra training that will come in handy and give you a boost on your journey. I know that can be hard to remember, especially when you are at one of those tough, downward parts of the squiggly line. Nonetheless, it's an important perspective to maintain.

## SQUIGGLY LINE STRATEGY: NAVIGATING THE VALLEYS

The times that we miss the mark are key opportunities for learning and growth. If we take the time to process these moments, respond to them appropriately, and reflect on the key lessons, we'll be better equipped as we continue on the squiggly line journey.

First there's an important mindset shift that we need to make. We have to stop fearing the worst and going into downward spirals of negativity when we make mistakes or experience setbacks. We're human. We're going to get it wrong sometimes because we aren't perfect. Not everything will go as we expect. What's most important is this: let's make sure that we're doing our best to conduct ourselves in a way that doesn't harm others or ourselves. If we use that as a guiding principle, then usually getting it wrong isn't such a negative thing.

When we do get it wrong, it's critical that we call ourselves on it. That can be really hard because it often means that we not only need to acknowledge it but also usually need to *do* something about it. And sometimes, the action that we need to take is really uncomfortable and difficult. Maybe it requires having a tough conversation where you admit a mistake that you made; or maybe it means leaving a job; or maybe it results in ending a relationship. Nonetheless, it's essential, and it's necessary. Running from or avoiding our mistakes will only lead to larger issues down the line. And when that happens, it usually forces us to address them in a much higher stakes situation. Let's agree to call ourselves on getting it wrong so that we can learn and get it right the next time.

Let's shift gears to looking at how to handle setbacks. Navigating setbacks require a slightly different approach. It's important to take a step back and recognize that what we wanted is not what's in front of us. And then we need to calmly re-focus on what we're trying to achieve and determine what (if any) adjustments need to be made and any corresponding actions that we may need to take. Experiencing a setback isn't always about needing to do things differently; sometimes, it just about patience, perseverance, and the right timing.

## THE BOTTOM LINE

Let me bottom-line this whole straight line versus squiggly line discussion: living on a straight line is like accepting someone else's checklist for your life and living according to that, while living on a squiggly line is like creating your own bucket list for your life and living according to that. The checklist isn't about who *you* are, what truly motivates *you*, what excites *you*, what *your* purpose is, or what *your* unique talents are. But that bucket list is!

If there's a chance to live a life you want—one that has meaningful success, fulfillment, and impact—then why not? If there's a chance to use your unique talents and innate strengths to help others and leave a positive impact, then why not? If there's a chance to change your trajectory and stop living on the straight line hamster wheel, then why not?

I was where you are right now. I had a choice to live by a checklist or by a bucket list, to live on the straight line chasing meaningless achievements or on the squiggly line pursuing meaningful success. I made the choice to live on the squiggly line, and I have never looked back.

Each day, in many moments and at many decision points, I continue to choose the squiggly line over and over again. This means that I am embracing imperfection and living in a way that is meaningful, joyful, and allows me to succeed using my natural abilities. Is it always easy? No. But I would choose this path over living a 60 percent version of my life based on someone else's idea of what I should be doing and pursuing lots of unfulfilling achievements. It's like choosing to experience the world in black and white rather than in full color.

What will you choose? Will you start embracing imperfection and live the life you want, or will you just continue to settle for safe?

You're still with me, so you're choosing the squiggly line, right? This is fantastic! I'm excited for you! Let's keep going!

Next, let's talk about where you are today and focus on embracing your squiggly line. After that, we'll start talking about the future of your squiggly line and how you can shape your path going forward.

## Chapter Three

# EMBRACE YOUR SQUIGGLY LINE

One of the hardest decisions I made was going into consulting after medical school rather than continuing on my path to become a licensed, practicing physician. Often, when someone learns that about my journey, I am asked a series of questions about whether I feel like I wasted time in medical school, whether I regret the path that I chose, and if I could still arrive at the same place if I had "just skipped" medical school.

The first time someone asked me those types of questions, I really had to pause and reflect. After all, it did seem insane (and uncommon) to expend such energy to get accepted to medical school, complete it successfully, and then go on to *not* practice medicine. With some thought,

I now undoubtedly know the answer to all of those questions: no.

I do not feel like I wasted time in medical school, I do not regret the path that I chose, and I do not believe that I would be the same if I had "just skipped" medical school. Did I know that this is where my journey would lead? No. But I'm glad that it has, and I am grateful for how my journey—my squiggly line—has shaped me and what I have learned along the way.

Here's the thing: choosing the squiggly line means that the journey is imperfect. It will not always end up exactly where you thought it would—but that is not a bad thing because it often ends up better than you could have imagined or expected. And that has certainly been the case for me. I have decided to focus on staying true to my vision of success, ensuring that I lead a life of meaningful achievement and using my talents to leave a positive impact. No matter where you find yourself on the squiggly line, what is important is to embrace where it has taken you and focus on how to shape the journey going forward.

So, let's talk about how to embrace your squiggly line. There are four key parts: mapping, perspective, acceptance, and learning. We will talk through each of those in a moment. But first, there's one other point that's important to mention. Embracing your squiggly line is not a one-time thing. There are many moments when you will need to pause and take time to embrace your journey, especially during some of the valleys when the going gets tough. If you need a quick way to remember the four steps, just think: the squiggly line is My PAL. Okay, let's dive into these four key parts.

### MAPPING

The first step is to map your squiggly line. This is critical because the act of writing out the different events, decisions, and turning points is incredibly helpful, powerful, and insightful. Sometimes, we forget important parts of our own story or how a certain event led to or resulted from something else. Also, mapping it out causes us to reflect on our past and present journey through a very different lens.

So, tactically, here's how you do this: you'll need to draw out a squiggly line and map the key parts of your life along the squiggly line. To help with this step, I've created a Mapping Your Squiggly Line section in the appendix. In that section, I give detailed instructions on how to map your squiggly line, and I've included extra pages with empty squiggly lines for you to use.

### PERSPECTIVE

So, now that you've mapped your squiggly line, you're ready for the next step: perspective. This part is all about taking a step back to fully see your squiggly line and acknowledge it for what it is. You have been on a journey. Recognize and acknowledge the many parts of your squiggly line. Perspective is important because it creates a fact base and outlines the path that you have taken. Perspective is not about overlaying any judgment or any applying any descriptors to your journey. It is purely about taking a moment to just look at how you got from there (where you were) to here (where you are now).

### ACCEPTANCE

Next is acceptance. This is all about understanding that you have shaped your squiggly line and it has shaped you. There are deliberate actions and decisions that you made to create your path. And there are ways in which the world—people, events, etc.—interacted with and impacted you along your squiggly line. As a result, you have come to where you are today. Accept that. At this point, you cannot change anything that is behind you... unless we really do figure out time travel! All jokes aside, it is important to be at peace with the past being behind you and accepting that, at this point, you can only change today and tomorrow. Yesterday is a *fait accompli.*

And there's a little more to this acceptance thing. It is important to hold onto the positive and let go of the negative. Take it easy on yourself. There are some moments that were not your best, and that's okay. You're human. Don't carry that negativity around on your shoulders. There are also some moments where you were absolutely incredible and did things of which you are very proud. That's amazing! Remember and hold onto those!

#### LEARNING

Last is learning. The focus here is on maximizing the juice from the squeeze. Here's what I mean: you've lived on your squiggly line and all of the experiences—both good and bad—have taught you something. Hold on to the lessons. Let yourself off the hook for making a mistake, but remember what it is you learned in that moment or the times that followed that mistake. And that really proud achievement? What did you learn about yourself or the way to overcome something that you want to take with you going forward? The more we take time to process our experiences and incorporate that learning into how we move forward, the better prepared we are for the next adventure on our squiggly line.

We moved through that quickly, but I hope that you've taken some time to map out your squiggly line and work through the process of embracing it, through perspective, acceptance, and learning. It's a worthwhile reflection. And as I mentioned earlier, the practice of embracing your squiggly line will be helpful throughout your journey.

One of the biggest learnings along my squiggly line has been to stop settling for safe. Making the decision to go into consulting after medical school (rather than a residency and practicing medicine) was really about choosing to follow my passion and my purpose. It also required following a path that was less "safe"—it was foreign, it was new, it was unexpected. And I was not sure exactly where it would lead. There are many other lessons that have helped me continue to choose the squiggly line and refuse to settle for safe.

In the next part of the book, I'll share the six key lessons that can help you along your squiggly line. I'll tell you the story of how each of those lessons came up in my life, how I struggled with each of them before overcoming them, and some useful tools that you can start using today. As part of the list of tools that you can start using, I have also included a couple of questions for reflection in each of the upcoming chapters. I encourage you to pause as you're reading through the book to think about those questions and how they may apply to any current situations or decisions that you're facing. Let's keep going!

*Part Two*

# STOP SETTLING FOR SAFE

## *Lesson One*

# STOP ASKING FOR PERMISSION (OR SEEKING VALIDATION) THAT YOU DON'T NEED

"You won't win," he said.

A few moments later after continuing an uninteresting and empty exchange of a few more words, I gracefully found a way to end the phone conversation.

*Wow,* I thought to myself. *That was completely deflating. What nerve!*

But the damage had been done. I had gone from being pretty sure I would run in the election and feeling good about the decision to doubting myself, fearing the worst, and wondering if I was crazy for even thinking I could win.

What was going on? Well, let's rewind a bit. I was nearing the end of my first year in business school. The day before the phone call, a second-year student (who I knew pretty well) had invited me to coffee to tell me about the upcoming student government elections. As he talked, I listened nonchalantly. Then he said: "Fallon, I think you should consider running for president."

I laughed it off and told him I'd think about it over the next few weeks. Then, he informed me that I didn't have a few weeks. I needed to decide if I was running, find a running mate (the president and vice president ran on the same ticket together), develop a written platform, and submit it all in the next ten days.

I let the idea sink in over the next day or so, and I started to get excited. The idea of being involved in improving the experience, not only for my classmates but also for future student classes, made me feel like there was an opportunity to have a significant impact. I still, however, had some concerns. The role was a very visible one. Lots of speeches at different events, heavy involvement in discussions with the administration, and lots of eyes on you at all times. It would be a very serious responsibility and undertaking.

As I thought it through, I felt like it was what I wanted to do, and I thought that I could serve the school and the student body well in that role. *But* I was still a little on the fence. So, that's how I ended up on the phone with the guy who told me I would lose.

Why the heck did I call him? Simple. I was scared and I wanted someone to validate the decision I was making. Did it work? Not even close. Instead, it sent me into a spiral of doubt and temporarily undid the decision I thought I had made.

To this day, I'm not even sure *why* he didn't think I would win. When I reflect back on the conversation, he just talked about how hard it was and that I would need to get votes to win (duh!) and how much of an uphill battle it would be.

So, let's look at the situation I had gotten myself into: first of all, I wanted someone to validate a decision I was making because I was scared. If that wasn't bad enough, I wasn't even thoughtful about *who* I called to try to get input on the decision I was making—and that took this situation from bad to worse.

There's a very fine line between seeking counsel or advice

from a trusted person and seeking validation of your decisions. It is incredibly important to understand when you need advice from someone else to help you along your path. And there is nothing wrong with seeking that. But you have to be very careful not to allow your decisions to be subject to validation-seeking and undue influence.

Here's why: not everyone that you encounter will be able to think objectively and solely in your best interests. It's almost impossible for *anyone* to do that 100 percent of the time. We are all human with our own experiences, perspectives, and biases. Although we try our best not to let that cloud our counsel, it invariably does. What's even worse is that when other people feel limited or have self-limiting beliefs, they will likely pass that on to you by projecting their issues. Then, you'll wind up carrying around their perspective (and, unknowingly, their issues) unless you work hard to resist adopting their beliefs. So, if you're not careful, what starts as an innocuous conversation exploring ideas and trying to solidify a thought or decision can be pretty damaging or defeating. And that's what was happening in that conversation.

It is important to have people that you can seek support from, but you have to be thoughtful in how you choose those people. You want individuals who can look at situations through your lens or context and provide a balanced perspective and wise counsel (and sometimes directly help!) to propel you along your path. That does not mean they will always say yes—this person will likely also challenge some of your assumptions, help you see things from different perspectives, and suggest different options to consider. And that's fantastic! That type of support will help you hone your evaluation and decision-making process while ensuring that you make the best choices possible with the information that you have.

You do not want to rely on people who will only tell you the negatives or always find the reasons that you cannot do something. If that happens, it is likely because of a negative past experience they've had themselves or they may be projecting their own fears or limitations onto you. It's also possible that they think they're protecting you by not encouraging you to do something, especially if it could be perceived as risky. Nonetheless, if you have someone around you who constantly gives you negative feedback, you should be very careful in how you interpret guidance from that person.

You also do not want to rely on people who will only tell you yes, only say what you want to hear, or always agree with you completely. That person may be holding back thinking it's better to tell you what you want (or what they think you want) to hear rather than what you need to hear. It can be difficult for people to give you negative feedback or challenge something you think when they believe it'll hurt your feelings. Often, it's because they don't want to be the bearer of bad news or because they don't want to jeopardize the relationship that they have with you. Nonetheless, if there is someone around you who consistently gives you an affirmative reaction, you should be very careful in how you interpret that person's guidance as well.

### HOW I STOPPED ASKING FOR PERMISSION (OR SEEKING VALIDATION) THAT I DIDN'T NEED

I had to take a step back from the conversation and refocus on *my* thoughts before the call rather than taking any of what had been said as fact. Specifically, I went back to thinking about why I wanted to run and what I hoped to accomplish for the school and for the student body. I also asked myself if I believed I was the right person for the job.

It was an incredible process and inner dialogue—and it had to happen fast! I had days to think through that and then find a running mate. In the end, I decided that I wanted to run for the position because I truly loved the school and my experience thus far. I wanted the opportunity to give back in service of my classmates and the school while partnering with the administration to create an even better learning environment.

Clarifying what I wanted and why was great. But there

was something else that I had to do: I had to let go of the outcome. I had to be okay with losing. If I thought it was worth it and that I was the best person for the job, I had to go all in and trust that my classmates would elect the person they thought would best fill that role. This was probably one of the hardest parts because it would be such a public effort, and—to be completely frank—it would have been really hard to lose so publicly after putting myself out there and going after something that I wanted. But I forged ahead. Within a couple of days of making my decision, I talked to a few classmates about the elections and found a great running mate. Days later, we submitted our platform and made our candidacy official.

There are moments when a single decision leads you to a completely different place in life because of the impact that certain experiences can have on you. The decision to campaign for student body president was absolutely one of those decisions. The year that I served in that role was one of the most formative years for developing my understanding of what good leadership is, the type of leader that I wanted to be, and how I wanted to lead.

It was such an incredible experience to work with the administration and our peers (we selected a cabinet to support various initiatives) to achieve the different goals that we had set during the twelve-month term. I was proud of the work that we did as a team.

During that time, there was a lot of growth, which means there were lots of tough moments. But there were also many really great moments, too! Overall, the role was a huge undertaking. But as I've said before, the most challenging situations that we face are the ones that will drive the learning from which we will most benefit. And this experience was no different.

What is perhaps most amazing is that I went into the role thinking about how I could serve and be an active part of changing the school for the better. I never expected the role would change me for the better, too.

I'm glad that I had enough conviction to go after it despite my doubts (and failed attempt at externally validating my initial decision). What a travesty it would have been had I stopped believing I could and never even tried...all because of someone else's opinion.

# QUICK RECAP: STOP ASKING FOR PERMISSION (OR SEEKING VALIDATION) THAT YOU DON'T NEED

## SQUIGGLY LINE STRATEGY

Start looking to yourself first for the answers instead of looking outward to seek validation.

## HOW TO GET STARTED

When considering a decision or action, make sure you are clear not only on what you believe is the best next step but also on why you believe that as well.

## QUESTIONS FOR REFLECTION

What are the feelings or situations in which you most tend to seek validation and why?

How can you learn to trust your perspective, and if you need some guidance in certain situations, who is the best person (or set of people) for you to seek that from?

## *Lesson Two*

# STOP CLOSING DOORS PREMATURELY

*Anything with pasta...oh, this one is perfect...*I thought to myself as I flipped through the cookbook. I was a few days into self-prescribed reclusion. I had a lot of life to figure out. In four months, I was graduating from school. But I wasn't sure what I was doing next. The natural path would be to go to residency. After all, I was a medical student, and medical students are physicians in training. So, to continue would mean to go to residency, maybe do a fellowship, then go practice medicine as a fully licensed and boarded professional.

I needed to make a decision: would I go to residency, or

would I go into the business world? It was scary. I had wanted to be a doctor since I was six or seven years old. I was literally at the doorstep of my childhood dream. Many would even argue that the hardest parts of realizing that dream were behind me. But now was the time to choose a door to walk through. And I wanted to be sure about the decision because it was an irreversible one. Or so I thought.

I needed a few weeks of introspection, mostly in isolation, to give myself the space to think. And to keep me from being alone with my thoughts (and from going stir crazy!), I decided to cook my way through a recipe book. I had always found something therapeutic about making food. And if there was ever a time I needed a calming effect to support my decision process, it was now.

For the next few weeks, I would spend a lot of time alone with my thoughts. I interacted with very few people, having conversations only with those who knew me best. They were people I felt I could count on to help me make the right decision—or at least remain neutral if they gave any guidance as I worked through it. My parents were incredibly supportive about giving me the space to find my way toward a decision that would make me happy rather than nudging or picking a path for me. And there were a few really great mentors and friends who also gave me phenomenal advice.

One person in particular gave me guidance that I would wind up using over and over again in my life. He was a faculty mentor for some of my research and a person I admired and respected immensely. His list of accomplishments was long. But what was most incredible was his ability to create multiple innovative solutions to any problem. It didn't matter if you had a question about what career move to make next or if you were trying to solve the issue of misaligned incentives in a fee-for-service healthcare system. He had a gift for seeing every situation through a unique lens.

His advice? Keep the doors open as long as I could. It was pure brilliance. It had never occurred to me that I could treat my decision as anything but binary. In my mind, I could open only one of two doors, and as soon as I walked through the one I opened, that was it—the other door would vanish, possibly forever. It was flawed logic driven by incorrect assumptions. I knew that choosing medicine first (i.e., going to residency right after graduation) didn't mean I would forgo business. But I had assumed that choosing business first (i.e., not going to residency right after graduation and getting a job) meant that I had to forgo medicine.

The problem? My flawed logic was closing doors prematurely. I couldn't see any other way. I was forcing the door to close on medicine long before it needed to, and

I was using false trade-offs to guide my decision making. Though the path back to medicine would be a little harder if I chose business first, it wasn't impossible. And I could pre-seed the path back to medicine now by taking certain actions to make sure that my open door was more than just a small crack.

The rationalizations that I was making out of fear reflect the same type of thinking that prevents many of us from taking *that* step—you know, the step that represents the thing that you've always wanted to try and that you believe is your true purpose. Here's why that thinking prevents us from taking that one step: because it makes that decision seem irreversible and much more risky than it actually is.

The point here is that most decisions along our path do not have to be binary—nor do they have to be scary. We make them *seem* that way. But keeping the doors open allows us to see decisions in a different light and create optionality. And maybe most importantly, it creates space for us to take *that* step.

## HOW I STOPPED CLOSING DOORS PREMATURELY

About eight weeks before graduation, I decided to pursue the business path instead of the medicine path. To this day, it remains one of the hardest decisions I have ever made. But thanks to the advice of keeping the doors open as long as I could, I was at peace and felt confident. It was as if I had said yes to both, and had given myself more time to figure out exactly what I wanted to do. By experiencing the business path, it would provide a more direct understanding of what that would look like and whether I preferred that or being back in medicine.

Before finishing school, I took the prerequisite board exams for applying to residency and spent enough time rotating in various specialties to know exactly what I would want to practice if I decided to come back. I also had discussions with really great supporters to understand how to re-involve myself in clinic, research, and more to pave the path back to residency if that was the final decision. And I knew the optimal timeline: ideally, I needed to decide within twelve months (and the sooner the better) whether I was coming back or not. The reason for the timeline was this: there is a ton of knowledge that you need to care for patients and to successfully train during residency. The "use it or lose it" principle definitely applies here: the longer I waited, the more time I would spend away from medicine without using all of the knowledge I had spent four years learning in medical school. That meant that the longer the gap between medical school and residency, the more time it would take for me to rebuild that full knowledge base, and the harder it would be to successfully transition back to medicine.

In the end, I would never actually go back to clinical medicine. I miss aspects of it even today, like the science of medicine, being able to help people so directly, and being in the operating room. But I know the decision that I made at that time was one of those critical steps that put my life on an entirely different trajectory. To be clear: I believe that practicing medicine is an incredibly noble and fulfilling profession, and I count myself very fortunate to have had the opportunity to make that my career. However, given the broader set of interests and passions that I had beyond medicine, it was not the best path for me to take. Understanding that and choosing a different path as a result of that realization was absolutely the right decision for me.

## QUICK RECAP: STOP CLOSING DOORS PREMATURELY

### SQUIGGLY LINE STRATEGY

Start learning to see and create optionality instead of forcing yourself to close the door on an opportunity that you don't have to decide on just yet.

### HOW TO GET STARTED

When making decisions, try to focus only on what you absolutely must answer or decide immediately. Look for options where you can leave the possibility or option open until you have enough information to confidently make a decision.

### QUESTIONS FOR REFLECTION

What are the doors that you can keep open while changing directions or trying something new?

What are the steps that you need to take to keep that door open?

## *Lesson Three*

# STOP COMPETING AND COMPARING

I was so scared. I literally woke up every day going to work thinking that I would get fired. It was my first job in a large, established company. And I had no clue what I was doing. Those first few months (and even longer than that, to be honest), I felt inadequate, and I thought that it would only be a matter of time before they sent me packing.

As if that wasn't enough, every day, I would question my decision to not go to residency and take the path into business. I would constantly ask myself whether I had made the "right" choice. And on the days that were especially difficult at work, I would tell myself something like: *See, you should have just done residency—you should have stuck to the original plan, to the original path.*

So, I had a two-part problem. Let's talk about the first part: I didn't know that it had a name at the time, but I was dealing with what was first described as the Impostor Phenomenon in the 1970s by Georgia State University researchers Clance and Imes. Today, it's often referred to as the Imposter (or Impostor) Syndrome. It's the feeling that you're a "fraud" and doubting yourself, your capabilities, and worthiness for your job or role.

Now, let's focus on the second part of the problem: I was comparing and competing against a different version of myself. And it didn't make sense because that other version of myself was nonexistent. Let's back up for a second: five months earlier, I had made the decision to try the business world instead of going into residency after medical school. And every day, I was trying to compare the level of success, achievement, and adequacy the business version of me was having compared to the medicine version of me...if the medicine version of me had actually existed.

There are *so* many things wrong with that picture. First, let's agree that competing and comparing yourself to anyone else is a fool's errand. You are absolutely falling into the trap of living someone else's vision and path instead of your own if you do that. And it only leads you to a negative place. Either you constantly feel inadequate trying to keep up and do the same things, or you are following a path that is not made for you and while you may be successful—to a degree—you'll likely be unfulfilled.

Now, there's this subtle, undermining competing and comparing that we do *with ourselves* that can be equally as dangerous, if not worse. And it's the trap that I had fallen into when I began my job and was afraid that I had made the wrong decision. I started using my other possible path in medicine as a barometer for how things were going on the path that I had chosen, especially when I was having a tough day.

Let me give you an analogy to show how nonsensical and completely unhelpful that was. Today, I rarely get in my car to head somewhere without looking at some type of navigation app that analyzes traffic and gives me the fastest route. One morning, I was heading to the airport, and I checked for the best route because it was the start of rush hour, and I wanted the app to tell me the fastest route based on the current traffic conditions and other factors (e.g., construction, car accidents). The app gave me a route that I don't usually take, but it said that was the best route and would get me to the airport in what I considered a reasonable amount of time. So, I hopped in the car and pondered whether I would follow the app's guidance.

About five minutes later, it came time to make the turn

that definitively accepted the alternate route that the navigation app had given me versus the route that I usually take. I hesitated for a moment. On the road ahead, I didn't see any traffic or anything that would lead me to believe that my usual route would be slower. And the navigation app wasn't showing me a direct comparison between the two routes, so I couldn't even compare them myself.

I decided to make the turn following the navigation app's guidance and trusting that it was the right decision. While on this "modified" route (the one the app suggested), on occasion I would second-guess whether or not I was truly saving time versus my "usual" route. But I dismissed the thought because there was no way that I could actually know what was going on or what would have happened on my "usual" route—because I was not there. There is no way to know how long the drive would have taken, if I would have gotten into an accident on the "usual" route, or avoided some sort of delay by taking the "modified" route. All I could do was focus on the path that I had chosen and be fully present. Comparing the "modified" route I was on to the "usual" route was impossible. And trying to compete against my "usual" route was also impossible. I have no idea how long it would have taken on the "usual" route versus the "modified" one I was on that morning.

Let's get back my job situation: the same logic applies.

The comparative "analysis" I was doing was ridiculous. I only had one life and one path, and that was the one that I was on. I couldn't do any type of real comparison to any other option at that point because it wasn't the path that I had chosen. There was no way to understand what successes or obstacles that I would have encountered had I taken the other path, because I didn't.

What's worse is that this competing and comparing thing just made the other path—staying in medicine—that I *wasn't* on seem like it would have been a better option when things got hard. Basically, I had the "grass is greener" syndrome. That was so unfair to myself. It was unhelpful, illogical, and deflating.

## HOW I STOPPED COMPETING AND COMPARING

One day, as part of the project that I was working on, I sat down for a feedback discussion with a senior project leader on my team. She happened to have a PhD, and she had also faced a similar decision when she chose to go into consulting instead of pursuing a career in research and academia.

As part of our conversation, she asked me about the transition from medicine and how I was doing. I decided to be completely honest, and I am so glad that I did. I told her that I was questioning myself for the decision and having a tough time adjusting. And I explained that every day I asked myself whether or not I should have chosen this path to try to gauge whether I was doing the right thing.

She smiled and then shared an incredible piece of advice based on how she evaluated decisions: her recommendation was to revisit decisions at a time interval that matches their magnitude. She then went on to explain what she meant: choosing medicine versus business was a big decision that had a big effect on my life and its direction; as such, I needed more time, data points, and reflection to fairly reevaluate that decision. And besides, I would likely just drive myself crazy thinking about it every day. Because it was of such a big magnitude, I needed to give myself bigger gaps in time to evaluate that type of question.

On the other hand, asking myself what I wanted to eat as a next meal was fine to ask often and without negative consequence. It was a small-magnitude decision with less impact on my life. I didn't need as much time, data points, or reflection to fairly evaluate that. And if I didn't quite like whatever choice I made, it was an easy change at the next meal—or even before! Because it was of such small magnitude, I could give myself much smaller gaps of time to evaluate (and reevaluate or change) my answer to that type of question.

That conversation completely changed my perspective.

From that day forward, I stopped second-guessing my choice every single day. And what a weight that lifted from my shoulders! Instead, I would evaluate the decision at intervals of six months or longer. I also started to accept the choice as my current path—one that I could change when I wanted—but the one that I had chosen to be on at that time. By accepting that choice, I also had to fully accept that there was only *one* me and *one* path. There wasn't some ghost of me out there on the other road that I didn't choose. And because of that, I also had to stop competing and comparing where I was...because there was nothing else to compete with or compare to!

Now, was I still scared because it was my first real job? Yes. But I learned to give myself the space (and the time) to develop and ask for help so that I did eventually know what I was doing. And you know what I started to realize? That was part of the point. I wasn't supposed to know everything automatically. Learning from others and developing my skills through the experience of working on different projects was all a part of the journey.

All in all, I was right where I was supposed to be. Yet, I had the ability to change my trajectory at any time. I did not need to compare my path to or compete with any other possible path. I just needed to focus on where I was and make adjustments to the future that I was heading toward whenever I felt the need.

## QUICK RECAP: STOP COMPETING AND COMPARING

### SQUIGGLY LINE STRATEGY

Start focusing on where you are, where you want to be, and how you can get there rather than competing with or comparing your path to other paths and reliving decisions that you have already made.

### HOW TO GET STARTED

Own your journey and make the changes necessary to impact your trajectory if you want to be on a different path.

### QUESTIONS FOR REFLECTION

What vision have you set for yourself and in what ways does your path and its future trajectory align (or not align) with that vision?

How will you personally measure what progress and achievement look like along your path rather than comparing them externally to define success?

## *Lesson Four*

# STOP WAITING FOR PERFECT CONDITIONS

"Well, no, that makes absolutely no sense," I said. I was in the car with a friend heading toward Decatur, a neighborhood east of metro Atlanta. We were talking about the vision I had for my career and what I *really* wanted to do.

"Why *not*?" my friend asked, a bit bewildered by my response.

"Just because. That's way too risky right now. I mean, I'm thinking about getting married and having kids in the next few years. That's just not a risk that I should take right now," I said. "It's just not the right time."

"Fallon, this *is* the time to take the risk," he responded. "It's not going to get easier later."

The risk we were talking about was trying to start a venture capital or private equity fund. For years, I had said that I wanted to create a fund that focused on investing in healthcare companies that innovate and improve healthcare globally. But to go do that would mean that I had to completely switch careers, find people to work with on this dream, and figure out how to forgo a steady paycheck for an undefined period of time.

But if we look back, there was actually a much bigger issue. I was deciding that because I was past my thirtieth birthday, marriage and kids were coming, and I needed to be prepared for that. I was risking *not* going after a dream for a relationship and family that I didn't even have and weren't even on the horizon. Why would I do that? Because that's what the life plan in my head said should happen. And on top of that, many people I knew were getting married and having kids...so it seemed like that was what I should be doing at that point, too. And I used that as the reason (or, more aptly, an excuse) for not being the right time to try to build a fund.

Looking back, I cannot even believe I was thinking that way at the time. It makes me cringe. And not only did I think it, but I also said it out loud, *and* I defended it. Holy cow! And, by the way, do you want to know what timeline I was using to judge when I should get married and have kids? Oh you know, the one that I created over a decade ago when I was a freshman in college planning out my life. And boy, was that timeline wrong. *So* wrong. (Flash forward to the future for a moment: over four years after that conversation, I would still be unmarried with no kids!)

If that wasn't bad enough, I was also playing quite a mind trick on myself. I kept talking about "risk" and "timing" but in reality, I was searching for the perfect conditions and creating reasons why that moment was not ideal... and all the while I failed to realize that no moment would ever be perfect.

Let's say it out loud together: there is no such thing as perfect conditions. Good. So, stop waiting for them. If they do not exist, then they will never magically arrive. And if they will never magically arrive, then waiting for that ideal moment to do something means that you never will go do whatever that thing is. Now, I know you're thinking: *But Fallon, there have to be better moments than others.* Okay, that's fair. But let's walk through this logic a bit.

I'll posit that while there may be better moments than others to take the leap, no single moment will be as ideal as we thought. Why? Because nothing goes perfectly according to plan. Why is that? Because perfect is impossible. So, even if you have the perfect business plan for starting a widget factory, inevitably, something will happen that you did not expect. Sure, you had all the capital investors lined up, all the employees you needed, the best suppliers, customer preorders, and distribution all set. But maybe one of the investors backs out or puts in less capital than expected. Or maybe it costs more to get the factory up and running, so you have to sacrifice investment elsewhere. Or maybe that one brilliant guy or gal who was going to run your factory operations takes another job offer instead. Do you see my point? Even with a perfect plan, conditions change. We live in a dynamic world, not a static one.

It is important to plan, and we should. But here's the thing: if we know things will shift around anyway, then why not just take the leap now? Perfect conditions don't exist, and even when we think that we've created the ideal set of conditions to go after an opportunity, there's no guarantee it will actually play out that way.

And here's the magical thing about not waiting for perfect conditions: it's possible that things turn out even better than we envisioned. But for that to happen, it requires us to take a leap. So, what if rather than waiting for perfect conditions (which is flawed since they don't exist), you get to 70 percent perfect conditions and you take the leap anyway?

Let's go back to the widget factory example. Let's say you moved forward with a plan to get you through the first few months, but you know that you'll need additional capital in month six to keep going. Rather than waiting until you have a full year figured out, you decide to press go. You have a solid business plan, great support for troubleshooting how to get past the six-month mark, and a few leads on additional investors that you're already working. Besides, you already have a strong (albeit small) team of employees lined up with solid suppliers, great distribution, and a couple of customers. Once you're up and running, maybe your customers order more than you expected. Or maybe now that you're out in the market with a tangible product, you're able to more easily get more investors on board. Suddenly, you have more cash flow than you expected, and you're not even concerned about additional capital for another eighteen months.

Here's what was different about the widget factory this time: rather than waiting for it to be perfect and having everything figured out, the factory launched with a solid plan and a way to mitigate some of what wasn't quite worked out. Also, notice one other point that's really important: solving one of the core problems (getting additional investment) proved to be easier after taking the leap rather than trying to get it all perfect before starting. That's something that I've found to be true in many situations. Sometimes, not having all the answers holds us back, but once we just start, we are better able to find what we need (or what we need more readily finds us!) if we just press go.

It's impossible to have all the data points and completely perfect conditions. So, rather than sitting on the sidelines never going after your big dream or idea because it's not the perfect time, commit to doing it a different way—the squiggly line way. Work on the plan to get it 60 to 80 percent of the way there, understand the gaps, mitigate the risks that you can, then just go for it!

### HOW I STOPPED WAITING FOR PERFECT CONDITIONS

I kept convincing myself that it wasn't the right time for years (literally!) before I finally decided to work on starting an investment fund. Truth be told, it was such a hard decision. At the time, I had a career with a clear path for progression and growing earning potential. Taking a risk on an idea that I had no experience with felt like a very crazy, very bad idea. So, it took almost two years to get myself there, ready to go after it. I worked through a paradigm shift in my mind that started with fully acknowledging what I wanted to go after (the fund) and believing that it was worth pursuing.

What exactly was it that won me over in the end? I had three big realizations.

## LIFE IS A LIMITED RESOURCE

My life was finite. It was not an unlimited resource. I had no idea how much time I had to do something "later," nor did I know with certainty how my life would unfold. Putting off this idea further than I already had ignored the importance of the present. I would also be letting go of a unique opportunity to go after something that I wanted to accomplish. Not only would there be no perfect moment to do it, but also, there was nothing really problematic about pursuing my idea at that moment either. So, why wait?

## NEVER KNOWING "WHAT IF"

I couldn't live with myself never having tried and never knowing if this big dream I had could have worked out. The reality is that I had to go after this thing to actually find out what would happen. If I sat on the sidelines creating excuses and never trying, I knew that it would be something I would always wonder about. I didn't want that feeling hanging over me. I didn't want to always wonder "what if." So, why leave myself wondering?

## HARD NOW BUT HARDER LATER

My friend was right in that it wouldn't get easier, and I knew that the longer I waited, the less likely I would ever be to try. The truth was what seemed really hard and risky now would likely only seem harder and riskier as more time passed. I had seen many people become more and more risk averse as they experienced growing earning potential in more senior roles with even greater career stability. I knew that I wasn't immune to that. Stepping away to try the fund at a later point would only make the decision tougher and seem even more daunting. So, why wait until it was an even harder decision?

Call it YOLO, call it FOMO, call it crazy. But those three realizations are how I got over waiting for the perfect conditions.

It was unreal. In less than a month, I made the decision to go after something that had merely been a thought in the back of my mind for years. Even after reaching that point, I debated internally for several days, trying to talk myself out of it. But within a couple of weeks, I decided to move forward and officially communicated my decision to leave at work. It was pretty abrupt when it all happened. But deep down I knew that it was time. I needed to go after my dream.

## QUICK RECAP: STOP WAITING FOR PERFECT CONDITIONS

### SQUIGGLY LINE STRATEGY

Start taking steps—no matter how small—that move you toward the thing you've always wanted to do or that idea you've been hesitating to try.

### HOW TO GET STARTED

Prepare and create a plan to make the conditions as ideal as possible, but don't expect (or wait) for everything to be perfect before pressing go.

### QUESTIONS FOR REFLECTION

What do you define as "perfect conditions" for that big step you're thinking of taking, and are they absolutely necessary to take the leap?

What is the minimal set of required needs that you must have before you try to do the thing that you've always wanted to do?

## Lesson Five

# STOP LETTING FEAR WIN

"Yes, and an ice cream cone please," I replied to the friendly cashier. I had just ordered some comfort food: chicken nuggets, fries, and ice cream. I needed it. As I sat down in the restaurant waiting for my order, I replayed the decision and rationale in my head.

*Okay...so I'm not taking this job. Right. And I don't have another job offer right now...but this one isn't right for me... and it's not my dream.*

I took a few deep breaths. I was trying to make sure I was buying my own story. My food arrived. I started to eat, but I was still in a deeply pensive state.

I had already given notice to leave my current job, and in two weeks, I would be formally unemployed. The week prior, I had received a job offer at a private equity portfolio company in the healthcare industry. The role would be in a strategy function as a director. Not a bad next step by any means. And for someone looking to go into private equity or venture capital, it couldn't be bad to get some operational experience at a portfolio company, I thought. But the job's responsibilities were much more than the director level title, the pay was not what it should have been for the set of duties the job required, and—perhaps most importantly—that job wasn't my dream.

My dream was to go start a venture capital or private equity fund with other MD/MBAs and invest in healthcare innovations. *That* was my dream, *that* was my vision. I had decided to leave my current job in pursuit of that singular goal. How could I have even begun to think of giving up on the dream so soon? Easy: I was afraid.

Fear is tricky. It's a double-edged sword. Fear has a necessary role. It helps us sense and understand danger, and when it's performing that function, fear can be protective. It can also help us understand when we are entering into uncharted territory—and likely on the verge of something big. In that context, fear is signaling that you're embarking on a new path, and that whatever it is you're going after is likely meaningful and important to you. Those are examples of the good side of fear.

However, there's a dark side to fear that can paralyze and derail. Have you ever gotten to a place (or ever seen someone else get to a place) where there is so much fear of what could happen that it becomes impossible to make a decision and take action? That's the paralysis. But there's something that goes a step further than paralysis: total derailment. And I was on the verge of succumbing to total derailment in this situation.

Fear, if we let it, can not only stop us in our tracks but it can also completely derail a plan or an aspiration. I was so afraid that I was about to let fear completely derail the path toward my big dream. I had already decided to pursue the fund and to leave my job—those were huge steps toward my aspiration. But with one decision, I was potentially going to abandon ship before I even really gave it a try.

When fear creeps in, it is important to call it out and understand whether it's performing a necessary function of protection, highlighting that you're embarking on a new path that you're passionate about, or preventing you from taking the next step by paralyzing or derailing.

Here are a few questions that I use to evaluate fear and

figure out how to move past it: What would I do if I knew that I could not fail? What's the best possible outcome by embarking on this path? What am I most afraid of if I embark on this path? Is there anything that would cause harm to myself or others (or requires breaking laws or not following my morals/values) by choosing this path?

After working through those questions with honesty, I can work through when I should pause because fear is being protective, when I should get excited because fear is signaling a new path and growth, or when I should hunker down and kick fear to the curb because it's serving as a detractor. And then, I also figure out how to solve for the things that are concerning me. In this case, fear was definitely serving as a detractor once I evaluated where I was. So, I had to figure out how to push forward past the fear.

### HOW I STOPPED LETTING FEAR WIN

Two days after my comfort meal, I turned down the job. I cried the morning after making the phone call to decline the offer. I was so afraid that I was making an irreversible mistake by forgoing a salaried position in pursuit of my dream. But I kept pushing ahead as I created a plan to help me move forward to address my greatest concern: cash flow.

Within weeks of making that decision, I founded a company while also working with a great friend and mentor on starting a fund. I did both simultaneously so that I could earn an income until the fund was far enough along. Here's a little more background on how starting a fund works and why I chose a parallel path: it takes time to be paid from running an investment fund. Typically, it can take one to two years for a brand-new fund to raise the money that it will use to invest in companies. Until at least a sizable portion of the fund's targeted fundraising goal is reached, the fund doesn't have the capital to pay salaries.

While gearing up to make my company profitable and working on the fund simultaneously, I used my savings and borrowed from my retirement plan to get the company up and running and stay afloat. I even moved out of my beautiful but crazy expensive apartment, put most of my things in storage, and lived with a friend for two months to give myself the runway to make it all work.

The path that I chose was not easy, but it was far more amazing than I could have imagined. And as I continued along my squiggly line, I knew that pursuing my dream—staying true to my vision and not letting fear win—was better than settling for the job.

Over the next eighteen months, the company I founded gave me incredible flexibility, an interesting variety of projects, and much higher income than I would have had in that director role. Amazingly, it became profitable within twelve weeks of founding, and it provided the financial stability and time that I needed to work on the fund. And finally, twenty-one months after I had said no to my not-dream job, the fund made its first investment in a company as a co-investment (meaning in partnership with another fund).

Was the story over and success declared on the fund even at that point? No, there was much further to go even after that milestone. The fund was still in the fundraising process to reach its target size. And after that was achieved, then would come the real work of selecting the right companies to invest in and supporting those companies in their growth while generating a return on the invested capital. Did I know how long it would take to get there? No. But I wanted to keep trying. And luckily, with my small business still going strong, I had the flexibility and cash flow to sustain myself as we continued to push forward. Nonetheless, I had taken a huge step in learning how to overcome fear.

## QUICK RECAP: STOP LETTING FEAR WIN

### SQUIGGLY LINE STRATEGY

Start using fear to drive you instead of letting fear deter you.

### HOW TO GET STARTED

Start by identifying each fear that you have around a particular situation or decision, then identify actions that you can take to address the fears or reframe the fears as growth opportunities (instead of seeing them as barriers).

### QUESTIONS FOR REFLECTION

What would you do if you had no fear of failure?

Where (or how) is fear paralyzing or derailing you right now and how can you move past the fear?

*Lesson Six*

# STOP LIMITING YOURSELF

"Fallon, what's the vision that you have for your business?" she asked me.

I paused. I was a little thrown off and at a loss for words, which is rare.

Then, she started to ask the question more pointedly. "In specific terms, what's the vision for your business, the clients it serves, how much it makes, and how much you want to make?"

It felt like such a big, complex question. But *why?*

I was in year two of running a profitable advisory business. I had consistent clients that kept returning to me for additional work. I barely did any sales or business development. I hadn't written a "real" proposal since I started the company. At that point, I really wanted to focus on the infrastructure necessary to grow the company further and become a larger, multimillion-dollar business. Or so I thought.

I fumbled through the rest of the conversation, sharing parts of the vision for the company around growth aspirations and the types of clients I wanted to serve. I was saying the right things. I was focused on the right things. If only that was truly what I wanted to do.

While the company had worked well, I wasn't excited about the work that I was doing anymore. To be honest, some days, I was really frustrated and uninspired. At times, I didn't feel like I was making a real impact or doing anything that was truly meaningful. Was I making money? Yes. Was I comfortable? Yes. Were my clients happy with the work? Yes. Was I grateful? Absolutely. But I wasn't fulfilled.

It took about a month of deep introspection (but no cookbook or food processor this time!) to take a step back, look at the business that I had created, and go "all in" on believing that I could grow it to be as successful as I wanted. Through that process, I acknowledged and appreciated the determination and strength it had taken to get the company to where it was—profitable, growing, and creating value for its clients. Although there were moments of difficulty, I had learned a lot in the process, and I could be proud of what I had achieved—especially as a first-time entrepreneur.

After embracing my journey to date, I also had to admit to myself that I was scared. It seemed like such a big goal. My eyes were set on creating an eight-figure business with a sizable team. As I took stock of what I truly wanted to achieve and what my goals were, I discovered something really interesting...and unexpected.

One week after Thanksgiving, I started to think about defining how I would ideally spend my time and what I was passionate about. Out of left field, it hit me: I actually wanted to do something completely different. I didn't really want to focus on building this company beyond where it currently was. I was interested in doing something else.

So, what was it that I really wanted to do? First, I started with outlining the key activities that would comprise an exciting and energizing day. I wanted to speak, write, learn, and read every day. I wanted to travel. I also wanted to create valuable content and to teach. I wanted the output of my daily activities to help people and have a positive impact. As I began to think about what I love to do and some of my innate talents, I translated this brainstorming into a more tangible path: become an internationally renowned speaker and author who focuses on inspiring others to live in their purpose, achieve meaningful success, and positively impact others.

Now, you may be wondering the following: *Well, Fallon, if that's what you really wanted to do, then why in the world were you so focused on building a completely unrelated business that you didn't even like anymore?* Here's the honest answer: I was afraid to admit what I wanted, the business I had was familiar, and I didn't believe that I could build a life out of what I loved. Let's take a look at each of those.

I believe one of the toughest things that we will ever have to do is ask and honestly answer one simple question: what do you want? Acknowledging and articulating what you want is hard for a couple of reasons.

First, the acknowledgment is tough because we've often told ourselves that it's impractical to want something or we've come up with a million reasons why we shouldn't want it. Or maybe other people have expressed those perspectives, and we have adopted them as beliefs. Furthermore, acknowledgment creates an attachment. It's easier to dismiss something if you've never admitted it was what you wanted. If you, instead, act like it doesn't matter to you, it hurts less if you decide not to go after it at all *or* if you go after it and fall short. Essentially, this is about avoiding a sense of loss and perceived failure.

Second, articulating what we want is also hard because it makes this fleeting thought something that is much more real. And when it's real and we've put it out there, it requires that we choose to act on it or not act on it. That's not necessarily an easy decision to face or to make. And living with the aftermath of the choice can be hard. Choosing to act means there's a next step of figuring out exactly how to do what you want or get to the goal that you want to achieve. It may be complicated and overwhelming. Choosing not to act means that we'll have to find a way to be at peace with the decision. That may prove to be particularly challenging, especially if we feel like we've foregone a big dream by deciding not to pursue what we want.

Beyond the difficulty of admitting and articulating what I really wanted, focusing on what was familiar felt so much better than going after an unknown. I was in my comfort zone. The business that I had already built was what I knew. And so far, it was working. I knew that I could make it even more successful because I knew exactly *how*. The whole speaking and writing thing? That seemed *way* out of my league. What made it even worse was that I didn't know how to do it. There wasn't a clear path.

But that wasn't all. There was one more thing holding me back. Deep down, I didn't believe that I could achieve what I wanted. I had never tried professional speaking or really thought of publishing a book before. And I certainly didn't know how to do that at a national or international scale. Sure, I knew *of* people who did that. But I didn't know them personally. And those people—they were *huge*! They were people like Oprah Winfrey or Brené Brown or others. For a moment, I didn't believe that I could be like them.

Not only was I scared, but I was also carrying around a self-limiting perspective. I knew what I wanted to do, but I was telling myself that I couldn't do it. And here's the real danger in what was happening: if I stayed in that frame of mind, there was no way I could achieve my goal.

## HOW I STOPPED LIMITING MYSELF

At this point, I could recognize one of the biggest emotions that was there: fear. I called it out, and I started to welcome it, because I knew it meant that I was challenging myself and entering uncharted territory. That was good. The fear was a signpost that I was pushing outside of my comfort zone. Only there would I be able to achieve something that I had never done before. So, while it felt uneasy (literally and figuratively), it was exactly where I needed to be if I was going to go after this big goal.

The other thing that I realized was that this new goal meant a lot to me. That's the other reason why I was so scared. There was something truly profound about choosing this new direction. It was not just about creating a new business and having a new job that I do every day. It was about starting to focus on building a fulfilling life that I love and how I could create meaningful impact by helping others. I truly believed that taking this new direction would place me squarely on the path of walking and living in my purpose. This was big. The stakes were really high.

Despite feeling incredibly excited and inspired, this new direction felt daunting. I knew the path ahead would be challenging and would demand a lot of me. It would require vulnerability and honesty and openness. It would require sharing where I had failed so that others could hopefully avoid some of the mistakes that I had made. It would require hard work to figure out something that I didn't quite know how to do. But if I could lean into the discomfort, figure out how to tread this path forward, and ultimately help others, then it would be worth it.

Next, I had to stop believing that I couldn't do it. I literally had to just eject that belief from my mind. It was garbage. And it would become a self-fulfilling prophecy if I never tried. So, the next step was to just start wherever I could. I began to take action through what I can now see was a three-part approach.

### FOCUS AND PLAN

I created a targeted set of goals for myself, and I also made a vision board to help keep me focused and encouraged. I posted the vision board above my desk, and I would occasionally add inspiring thoughts or phrases that I encountered as I moved forward with my plan. In addition, I created a timeline for each of my major goals, such as writing this book and putting myself out there to speak at more events. At times, the deadlines I gave myself were way too aggressive and became overwhelming. I had to learn to be flexible and patient with myself. But I made sure to balance that leeway with firm deadlines for certain smaller milestones along the way to ensure that I remained committed and continued making progress.

### LEARN THE ROPES

I pushed myself to learn how to build a career in speaking and writing by seeking out everything I could find, from searching on the internet, to reading books, to asking friends who had worked in industries that required similar know-how. For example, I had a friend who was a genius in the consumer/retail space, and I asked her to help me understand how to think of myself as a brand and what I needed to do to create and build a consistent brand presence. I made some investments in a couple of courses, and I also began working with a coach to learn more about the speaking industry.

## ENLIST SUPPORT

I enlisted my tribe to go on the journey with me by sharing my goals and progress along the way. This group celebrated the small victories with me and helped keep me going when I felt defeated, crazy, and wanted to just quit. This group also served as a great testing ground for ideas that I was working through, like the initial outline for this book. It was amazing to have a safe space to share the work that was so personal to me as well as to get the feedback that I needed to make improvements on the content that I was creating.

So, what came next? I committed to finishing this book and getting myself out there to speak. I began sharing my new vision with others (beyond my tribe of close friends) so that they could help me identify opportunities to speak. Some even helped with editing this book!

I also closed my first business—the one that I originally thought I would grow into a larger company—because I knew that I wasn't passionate about that work anymore. I didn't want to waste my energy on something that wasn't meaningful or fulfilling. It was a scary decision since this new direction wasn't revenue-generating just yet, but I knew that I had to take the leap. And how exactly did I know? There was a certain joy and energy that I felt when I was speaking and writing that was just inimitable. I was in the flow. It came easily, and I loved what I was doing.

I had to think about the practicality of making money to sustain myself, but beyond that, I would do it even if I wasn't paid. I just couldn't imagine going back to spending my time doing things that I wasn't passionate about, things that weren't part of my purpose. I also knew that the business would be there. If something didn't quite work on this new path, I could go back to the old business if I had to—but I was really hoping that I would never need to.

What happened after all of that? Well, this part of the story is still in progress. It's my current adventure on my squiggly line, and I'll continue to share where it goes and what I learn along the way! You can keep track of my updated squiggly line on *www.OwnYourSquiggly.com* where I'll share what's happening!

But here's what I do know: all of the moments leading up to now have prepared me for this phase, and I'm thrilled (and, at times, a little scared) to be right where I am! The path may not always be clear, but I have a vision that excites me, and I'm taking bold steps toward it each day. But the *first* and most important step was to stop limiting myself and to believe that I could do it.

## QUICK RECAP: STOP LIMITING YOURSELF

### SQUIGGLY LINE STRATEGY

Start thinking and envisioning without limits; start betting on yourself and believing in your capabilities.

### HOW TO GET STARTED

Adopt a perspective that believes everything is possible if you are willing to create the path toward achieving your goal and believe in your capabilities.

### QUESTIONS FOR REFLECTION

What have you always wanted to do but have never tried to do?

What is the legacy or impact that you want to leave behind?

# CONCLUSION

## OWN YOUR SQUIGGLY

As I was preparing to write the last chapters of the book, I read about a speech that Oprah Winfrey gave. It was incredibly inspiring. As part of that speech, she talked about the mantra that she lives by: “Everything is always working out for me.” I wrote down the mantra on my vision board, and I made it a part of the way that I respond to any of the difficult moments that confront me along my squiggly line.

She then went on to say something that I found to be equally powerful and also incredibly true of my own journey: “Look at how many times you were worried and upset—and now you’re here today.”

She was *so* right. Here's what I have experienced and believe to be true: throughout life, things will happen *for* you, not *to* you. Every moment is a reflection of where you are, what you can learn, and how you can grow—especially in the times that are the toughest. Just remember that if you hang in there, it will all work out for you, and in fact, it already is. There's no reason to get upset and worry, because it is part of the squiggly line.

*Life Is A Squiggly Line* has focused on embracing imperfection and not settling for safe. And during our time together, you let me (hopefully!) help you decide to live life on the squiggly line.

Now, it's time for you to go out there and own your squiggly! What does that mean? Well, there are three parts to it.

## BE BOLD!

Set a clear vision for where you want to go and ensure that it aligns with your passion and your purpose. It's okay for the vision to shift or change as you continue along your squiggly line. It's natural for your vision to evolve over time as you have different experiences that expand your perspective. Just make sure that the vision is always true to you.

**BE BRAVE!**

Take steps toward your goal and embrace the fact that the journey won't be perfect—but keep going anyway, and learn from the successes and challenges that you encounter.

**BE YOU!**

Use your unique talents and strengths to propel you on your journey, and create *your own* path toward *your own* vision...and enjoy it!

There's something else that I want you to know. Not settling for safe and owning your squiggly will be a journey in and of itself. In this book, I've talked about the six major lessons I've learned, and the situations where they most poignantly showed up in my life. But there are times where I've re-encountered those lessons (even after I thought that I had *really* nailed them) and have struggled to make the best decision for me...despite everything that I know to be true.

So, I'll add a seventh and final tip: stop being so hard on yourself. Allow yourself the room to make some mistakes and continue to grow. Perfect is impossible. It's okay to be human. We all are. Just promise that you'll keep going, that you'll keep learning, that you'll keep focusing on the overall journey. Because, in the end, that's what owning your squiggly line is all about.

I'm excited for you and what lies ahead! If you need help along the way, I'm happy to support you!

You can visit the website for tools that help you with the major topics we've discussed in this book and more. Go to *www.OwnYourSquiggly.com.*

The website also has information for you to get in touch with me directly!

I look forward to hearing all about how it goes! Please feel free to reach out to share your stories and successes—I can't wait to hear them!

Until we meet again on the squiggly line,

Fallon

# APPENDIX

## MAPPING YOUR SQUIGGLY LINE

In Part I of the book, I talk about embracing your squiggly line, which is a four-part process that begins with mapping your squiggly line.

As we think about our life experiences, there are three main categories that key events and actions fall into: self, personal, and professional. I'll define each of those.

### SELF

This category deals with realizations, perspective shifts, or educational pursuits that impact your life philosophies, change how you approach situations, give you additional skillsets or create other types of growth. The key is that the focus is solely on you rather than on your interactions with others or your pursuit of a career.

## EMBRACE YOUR SQUIGGLY LINE

Here's a condensed recap of the four key steps to embracing your squiggly line. For more detail, refer back to Part I of the book.

1. **Mapping.** The first step is to map your squiggly line. This is critical because the act of writing out the different events, decisions, and turning points is incredibly helpful, powerful, and insightful. Sometimes, we forget important parts of our own story or how a certain event led to or resulted from something else. Also, mapping it out causes us to reflect on our past and present journey through a very different lens.

2. **Perspective.** So, now that you've mapped your squiggly line, you're ready for the next step: perspective. This part is all about taking a step back to fully see your squiggly line and acknowledge it for what it is. Perspective is not about overlaying any judgment or applying any descriptors to your journey. It is purely about taking a moment to just look at how you got from there (where you were) to here (where you are now).

3. **Acceptance.** Next is acceptance. This is all about understanding that you have shaped your squiggly line and it has shaped you. It is important to be at peace with the past being behind you and accepting that, at this point, you can only change today and tomorrow. Yesterday is a *fait accompli*. Acceptance is also about holding onto the positive and letting go of the negative.

4. **Learning.** Last is learning. The focus here is on maximizing the juice from the squeeze. Here's what I mean: you've lived on your squiggly line and all of the experiences—both good and bad—have taught you something. Hold on to the lessons. Let yourself off the hook for making a mistake and celebrate the successes. The more we take time to process our experiences and incorporate that learning into how we move forward, the better prepared we are for the next adventure on our squiggly line.

### PERSONAL

The focus in the personal category is on personal life, which includes relationships with family, friends, partner/spouse, children, religious groups, and more. This will also include volunteer activities and any community engagement opportunities that you undertake.

### PROFESSIONAL

This category deals with career pursuits and aspirations. This covers a range of topics from your current job or the role that you want to pursue next to your professional network and that entrepreneurial idea that you're looking to launch.

I've defined these three categories so that when mapping your squiggly line, you can assess if you've focused on one area more than the other.

While we may emphasize one part of our lives more readily—for example, maybe you initially think more about the professional side but less about the personal—the reality is that we are a product of the collective experiences across all three of these categories. So, as you take the time to map your squiggly line, I recommend that you spend time thinking through all three of these categories to ensure the key pieces from each area are represented on your squiggly line.

Now you're ready to map your squiggly line! Below are some instructions that you can follow to help you with the mapping. When you're ready, go to the next page so that you can get started! Also, I've included a few blank pages for you to use—use as many as you need, but don't feel obligated to use all of them!

Quick start guide to mapping your squiggly line:

1. **Determine the start and end dates for your squiggly line mapping.** You can decide to use a year or a specific day for your start or end dates. You can map your entire life or just a certain time period. The mapping is all about what's most helpful to you. If you've never evaluated your entire life or a large portion of your life before, I'd recommend mapping over a longer timeframe. However, if you're really interested in a specific period of time where you made lots of decisions, experienced lots of changes, or navigated many transitions, then you can focus on a shorter timeframe instead.
2. **Write the start date at the bottom left corner of the squiggly and the end date at the upper right hand corner of the squiggly line.** If you need multiple pages to give you enough space to capture everything, then make sure you note the start and end on each squiggly line to help orient yourself.
3. **Start mapping!** You can begin by jotting down

whatever comes to you or you may choose a more structured approach, such as mapping by segments (e.g., start by mapping all self, then all personal, then all professional). Be sure to take a fluid approach. I find that when mapping my squiggly, I started chronologically then went back and added details here and there as I remembered them.

4. **When you're finished, go back to Part I of the book to move to the next step: Perspective.** After that, you'll move through two other steps in the process of embracing your squiggly line.

If it's helpful to see an example (or if you're just curious to see what's on my squiggly line), go to *www.OwnYourSquiggly.com* to see my squiggly line mapping. I'll also keep it updated as I have new experiences, so be sure to check back often to see how it changes!

# YOUR *Squiggly* LINE

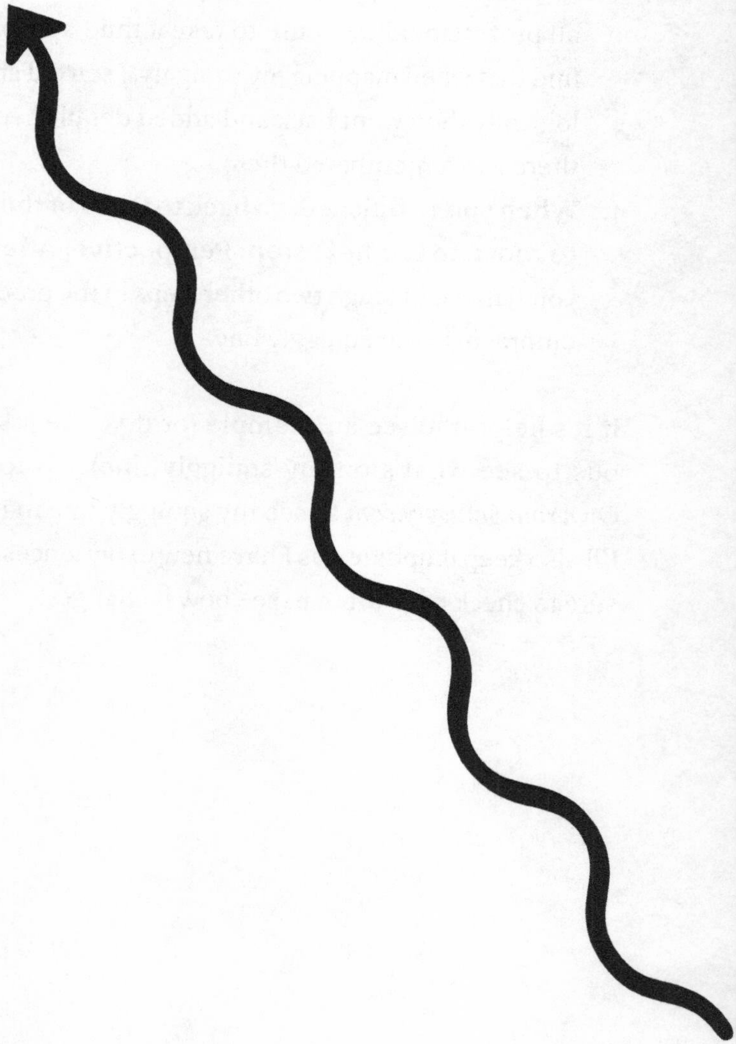

# YOUR *Squiggly* LINE
(continued)

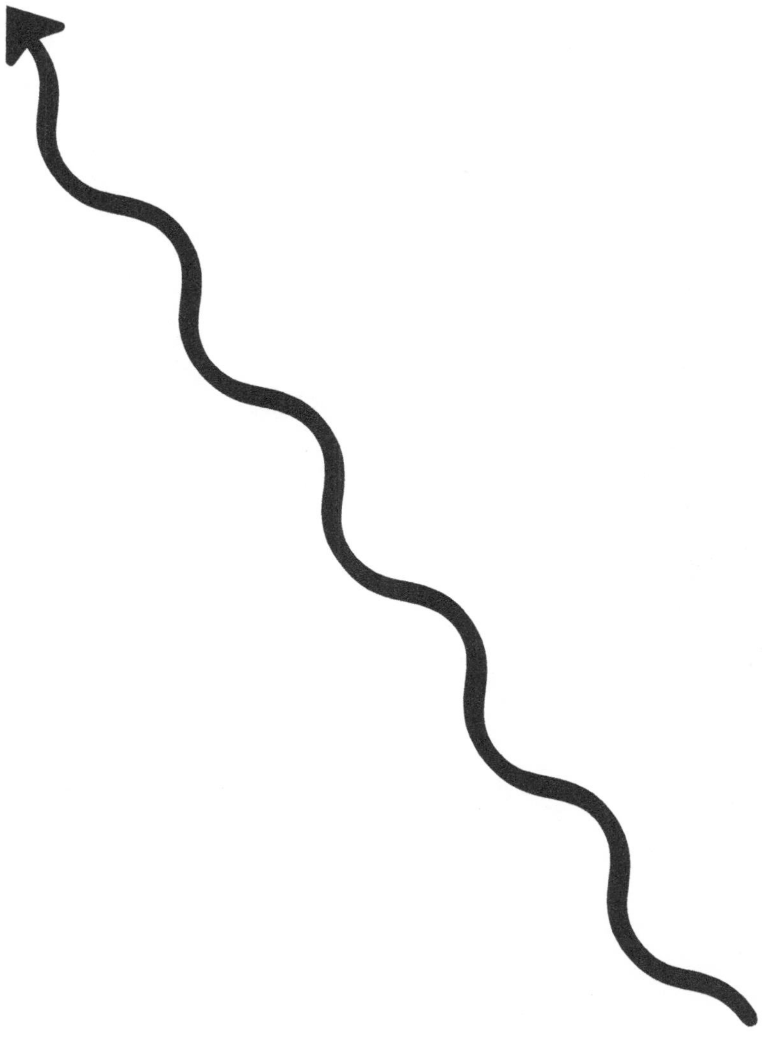

# YOUR *Squiggly* LINE
(continued)

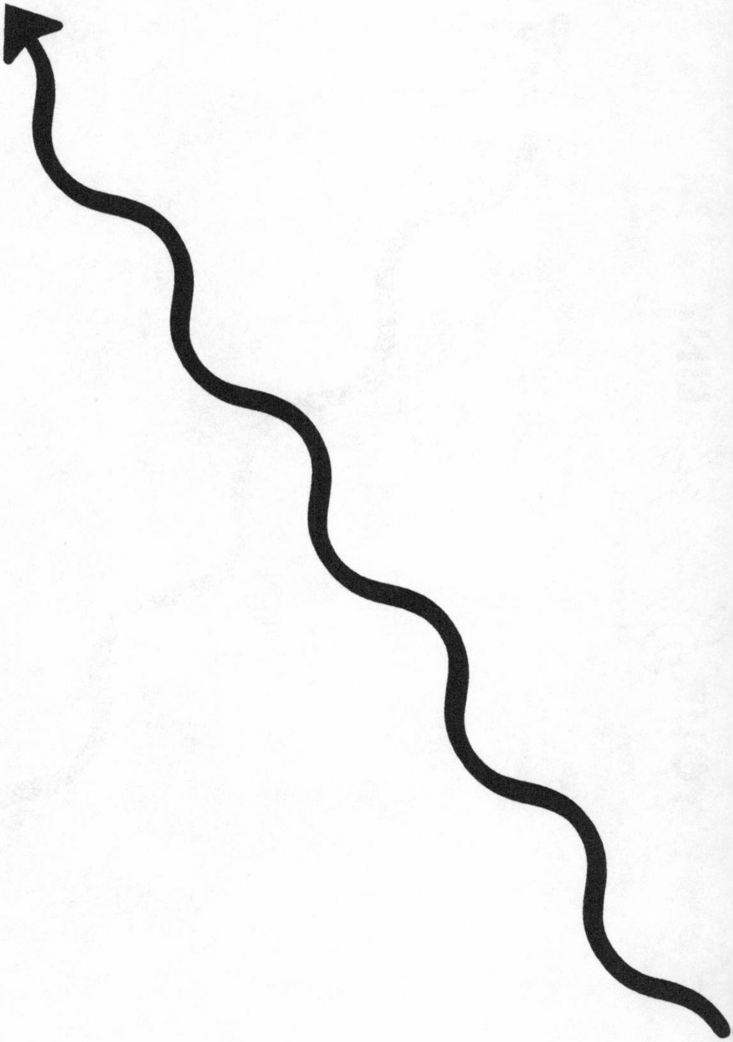

# YOUR *Squiggly* LINE
(continued)

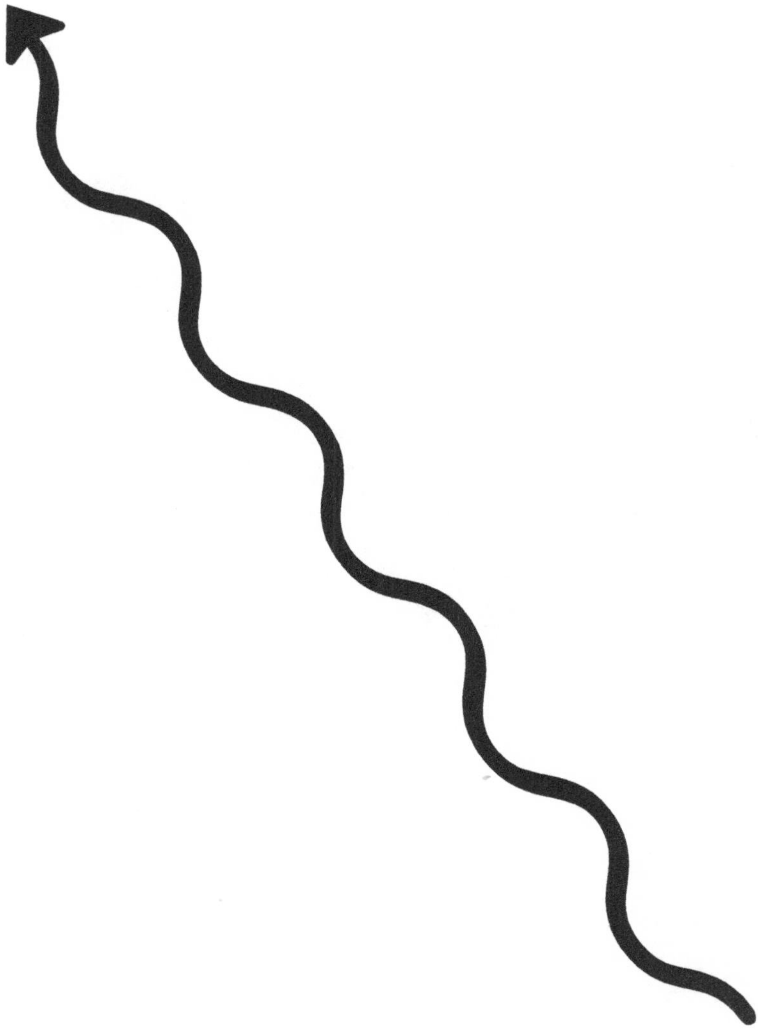

# ACKNOWLEDGMENTS

I am grateful to God for all that He has given me and for His loving guidance and blessings along my squiggly line. I am also grateful for such an incredible and loving family. To my Mom, Dad, and my brother, Shelter: I am thankful each day for the love that you all have given me, teaching me to keep God first, for helping shape me into who I have become, and for always reminding me that anything is possible.

I have been supported in bringing this book to fruition by a group of people who have helped keep me on track and excited at each step along the way, and I am very grateful for their help (and gentle pushes!) to make this book a reality:

*Alison Beavers, Jasmine Burnett, Wendy Ellin, and the Scribe publishing team*

I have been fortunate to have so much support along my journey from many amazing people. It would require an entire book to include all of those who have touched my life, and I am truly grateful to each of them for being an endless fountain of encouragement. I would like to especially thank the following people:

*Pamela Agava, The Agir Family, Emmanuel & Mary Ahua and Family, Ember Ahua, Rossie Ahua, Stacy Ahua, Moses & Angela Asom and Family, Emeline Aviki, Kelvin Baggett, Tom Barkin, Darius & JoAnn Bates, Erin Beasley, Alison Beavers, Barr Blanton, David Bueno, Joe & Tiffany Burns, Carolyn Day, Marc Ellis, Teresa Erold, Vivian Estes, Britney Fields, Dave Frank, Misa Fujimura-Fanselow, Laura Furmanski, Kimberly Futrell, Pastor Jim & Carolyn Giannantonio, James Goodyear, Jeet Guram, Alex Harris, Katie Hindman, Atalie Jacobs, The Kpamber Family, Jonathan Lack, Kate Lambert, Nicole Layne, Andrew MacDonald, Lynette Mark & Jim Michelson and Family, Shaden Marzouk, Sophie Masure and Family, Jennifer McKeehan, Linda Miller, Nichole Miller, Wendy Miller, Mayen Orok, Jai & Swati Parekh and Family, Selene & Zankhna Parekh and Family, Jean & Sophie Remy and Family, Liz Riley, Angella Rowe, Kevin Schulman, Matt Schroeder, Blair Sheppard, Valerie Skinner, Mark Stern, Roy Tapley & Robert Briscoe, Casey Taylor,*

*The Uganden Family, The Ukpe Family, Kathryn Valentine, Zakiya Whatley, Chikoti Wheat, Delbert Wigfall, Leviathan Winn, and Kneeland Youngblood*

I have been fortunate to attend incredible educational institutions and be part of amazing organizations and communities that have impacted my journey and helped me grow tremendously. I am grateful for how they have each shaped my path:

*Duke University (the Fuqua School of Business and the School of Medicine), Johns Hopkins University, McKinsey & Company (especially the Atlanta and Southern Offices), Young Women's Leadership Forum (YWLF), and the Kinkaid School*

I am grateful to have a group of fantastic women who have been mentors, coaches, and role models to me, without even knowing it! Thank you for boldly paving the way and for being such an incredible inspiration. I hope to one day have the opportunity to convene this amazing group of ladies for brunch!

*Brené Brown, Ariana Huffington, Michelle Obama, Sarah Jakes Roberts, Bozoma Saint John, Gabrielle Union-Wade, and Oprah Winfrey*

# ABOUT THE AUTHOR

**FALLON UKPE, MD, MBA** is a speaker, author, and entrepreneur whose mission is to live boldly and reach her highest potential while inspiring and teaching others to do the same. By doing that, she believes that we can all lead more fulfilling lives, achieve meaningful success, and create a lasting legacy of impact.

Fallon knows a lot about managing life's "squiggly line," having navigated four distinct career paths and two professional degrees by her early thirties. She has been mentioned in the *Financial Times* and published in *Shanghai Daily*.

Prior to launching her own businesses and writing *Life Is A Squiggly Line*, Fallon was a management consultant at a global consulting firm where she served healthcare, non-profit, and private equity clients in the United States, Europe, and Africa.

A native of Houston, Texas, Fallon earned a BA in French and Spanish from Johns Hopkins University in 2007, and then she completed an MD/MBA at Duke University's School of Medicine and Duke University's Fuqua School of Business in 2013.

Currently, Fallon lives in Atlanta, Georgia with her beagle, Riley. She enjoys volunteering with organizations focused on at-risk youth, education, and women in entrepreneurship.

To see the latest content and updates from Fallon or to contact her, please visit her website:

*www.TheOfficialFallon.com*

CPSIA information can be obtained
at www.ICGtesting.com
Printed in the USA
FSHW011135051019
62635FS

9 781544 505541